Fog and Woodsmoke

Fog&Woodsmoke
behind the image

EDITED BY Stephani Schaefer

Lost Hills Books
WWW.LOSTHILLSBKS.COM

Cover art: photography by Stephani Schaefer
Cover design: Aaron Bosanko
Interior layout: Aaron Bosanko

Published in the United States

ISBN 10: 0-9798535-6-7
ISBN 13: 978-0-9798535-6-2

Lost Hills Books
P.O. Box 3954
Duluth, MN 55803
WWW.LOSTHILLSBKS.COM

little song

a song in the kitchen
i heard her singing

tremulous with uncertainty
a thin little lyric
abandoned
tentative and alone
left in the unused
cupboard, i think it was

trying to sing itself home

                    —eric nystrom

CONTENTS

Blackbirds at Dusk

Flooded Road

Fog and Woodsmoke: Behind the Image

A man steps forward out of fog. What stories does he bring? How does he come to be? As you gaze at the man and at the fog, a few tentative words begin to form... they form as you look out and look in at the same time. You look in to a private set of associations gathered over years of living and reading.

We save images in many forms: drawings, post-card art, poems, paragraphs. We pin them to the fridge and bulletin board, tuck them into notebooks and memory. We make our selections of what to add to our internal world, and then we make up stories to explain what we see and what we keep—a set of endless permutations.

What interests me is the way in which we find connections between many separate things, how we each patch together our own collage. I was enormously pleased to get work that treated the photos as a group: Alan Catlin's Still Life with Dead Zone, Rob Davidson's Walter: Five Meditations, and Lyle Daggett's Flood Warning.

If a photo can go looking for words, words can call for a photo as well. Coming on the scene "Pavement Ends," I thought: there is Louis Jenkins' Mudhole, I must take that home. Taking things home is what I do: my photos are found objects and so is someone's poem posted over my desk. They are part of my collage, as are a few other previously published pieces included in this collection that, to me, have a natural home with these photos.

I like to take pictures at dawn and dusk, in rain and fog,

where what you see and what you feel changes with the changing light. For this project I selected ten photos that seemed to promise stories and then asked early responders to vote on which were most evocative for them. As it turned out, the five chosen make a portrait of my neighborhood, from Josephine Street to the back road I wander daily with camera and notebook.

The mind at work is a kaleidoscope where many bits and pieces fall together, then shift and change when we take in something new. This is the root of invention, how we leap to another place. A piece that mentions no detail of a photo may yet be intimately tied to it. Andrei Guruianu's poems make a direct and visceral leap to the heart of each image while embracing the whole.

Making this book was like making a poem: at the outset you exclude nothing, you let it grow from the ground up like bindweed after rain. Later, you make the hard decisions, what to keep, what to let go. I looked for quality and variety. I looked for pieces that had a kinship with each other. And I looked for work that brought together the interior world and the contemplated object.

Alan Catlin's piece is a rich example of this. The work is a set of five haibun: two prose poems linked by a haiku. In the first he contemplates the photos and in the second he gives us a series of war images, so that the effect is of one superimposed on the other, as when soldier or civilian must live with the after-images of war. They remind me, when I walk the back roads in contemplative quiet, that everywhere there are others who don't have this comfort.

William Stafford said, "Each person has need, each person will die, each person stares out of a story full of suspense and mystery." I looked for that. This book is a collage of found images, a chorus of voices with an established kinship, an open conversation. I hope you find things here to take home that may lead to new work of your own. If that happens I'd like to know.

Stephani Schaefer

FOG AND WOODSMOKE

Andrei Guruianu

Holdout

What haven't you lost yet?
With your gun unholstered in the dark.
What do you still believe in?
　　—these rivers ripped into the blacktop,
　　　craters of what passed before
　　　before it passed you by.
And now the dense fog of night.
These blistering lights
about to go out one at a time.

Flashlight Story 2

The air after rain. The sounds of lovers
making love, tea, toast, and nevertheless
going about their days. It has something

to do with gravity. One moment you're walking
at the edge of a street, when your brother
is taken from your hand. You go your whole life

thinking, Why him and not me? You wake
and are no longer young. Traffic is still insidious,
but now the hours come apart like soft-boiled eggs.

You spoon the round bellies out, pour on Tabasco,
grind fresh pepper, eating the moments so they
sizzle in your mouth, so they burn as they go down.

It takes a kind of courage, sometimes, just to say it.
Whole days spent otherwise have proven this to me.
Step forward, and the wind braces you on all sides.

Stephani Schaefer

Fog and Woodsmoke

Walking into a new year
through woodsmoke and fog I don't believe
there can be evil in the world.

Or I believe the sweet breath
of so many still sleeping is what makes halos
around each point of light.

At least this year
I don't find it in my own black heart, don't
read it onto the page before me.

Through this morning as soft as goosedown
I walk open handed
toward the door that opens daily in the east.

Judith Pacht

Surface

Like a motel, the table by the bed,
the dressers, veneer, everything
matching, serene and restful as motels
are meant to be, for the business traveler
who clinches a merger, the hungry lovers
who clinch and merge,
the invisible room
service, the waiter's smile as he enters
each opened door,

although you know, some days
with an ear to the facing, you can hear
the plywood peeling strip by strip,
the glue melting, dissolving to liquid,
and in a wind the water roils oily black
or turns viscous, even tears the heart,
all the while the veneer's shining smooth,
the grain unmarked,

and who would know, or even care, unless you prized
something solid, something durable, unless you counted on it.

Donna Pucciani

Distances

Barely visible, a distant human,
smaller than a fingernail, walks ahead
in the fog. The only clear thing tonight
is the cracked pavement of a broken street,
swallowing the foreground where I muse
with my camera, listening to my breath,
smelling incipient rain hovering above
newly exposed spring soil.

A streetlamp corona lurks
in the branches of floating trees,
where telephone wires hang heavily
on poles, filled with the hidden voices
of small-town America. The walker,
several blocks ahead, seems almost immobile,
a black stick insect clinging to the striated bark
of night. We are smitten by the scent
of dying embers, leaves curled into piles
of ash, gutters of dead vegetation.

Like me, he walks alone past triangled roofs
of modest homes, their windows dark,
their inhabitants turning in their beds
dreaming of children or snow or
falling off a mountain in Tibet. A certain
sadness nests in the heavy humidity
of dank soil, twigs furred in lamplight.
I will never meet the lone traveler ahead,
never shake hands with the man who inhabits
the house on the corner or wave
to his kid on a bike tomorrow or ask his wife
why the street is named "Josephine."

I don't know the neighbors well enough
to ask them to check my mail when I am
away. And when the fog lifts tomorrow
life will go on as usual
except for the guy three houses down
who has died in his sleep. The man up ahead
will have disappeared, and the bright sun above
will clarify nothing.

Walking in Fog

Where could that man go, this time of evening,
bundled against the cold? I've walked that way
in better weather. Someone stopped me, asked

was I looking for the homeless camp. No.
I simply wanted to be left alone.
Bundled against the cold, I walked that way

then turned back home. In town, I have four walls;
I've paid my bills and listened to the news.
I simply wanted to be left alone,

to see how clouds change a familiar view,
then pass beyond the dead-end barricade.
I've paid my bills and listened to the news,

and yet, who knows? Fog and muffled thunder—
and what light? I might have listened harder,
then passed beyond the dead-end barricade

to find what's waiting at the edge of town.
In better weather, someone stopped me, asked
for what? Light. I might have listened harder.
Where could that man go, this time of evening?

In the Streets

He carries everything he owns in a paper bag. What are you? A broken alarm clock? A returnable pop bottle? Once, on this very corner, a man hit him in the mouth. That's why some of his teeth are missing. It was drink that made that man hit him. He never drinks. He waits for you every day with his hand out. Every day without fail. It's a wonder he's still alive. The coldest days he spends at the public library. But where does he go at night? The moon is shining now at four in the afternoon and down here it's all wind and shadows. In the streets with the blowing snow and newspapers he carries on the same argument with his parents, though they have been dead thirty years. At the mouths of alleys he pauses… He is an only child. All he wants is his share.

Nancy Paddock

In the Dark of Morning

Dreams are fragile as a spider's web
blundered into by moonlight,
the pattern torn, threads drifting.

Sometimes nothing is left but the ghost
of a certainty that something insubstantial as mist
and vital as the heart's cadence has been lost.

Messengers from the other world—
speaking in tongues of flame, of blessing
or curse—dreams scribble poems
in frost feathers on a darkened window,
hide riddles that must be solved
in broken bottles, their ink washing away
in a tide of wakefulness.

In the harsh daylight world of cause and effect,
of duty, logic, and solid substance,
the dream—no matter how real—may perish
as snow drifts away with the wind. Yet

on these frail wires we suspend our lives—
these cryptic messages scrawled
on tide-washed sand, or in the gauzy cloud
our breath leaves on a mirror.

Crossing Josephine

Three streetlamps suspend
over the road in fog
so heavy it cannot lift
itself above the wires,
an atmosphere more visible
than the blocky figure

passing the solitary

house with its roofline
edged ember-white.
Obstinate, unseasonable,
the strung lights form
a mountain range, triple
peaks touched by invisible sun,

fog-saturated, incapable of heat.

What echoes in his head –
artillery of words, siren
of an infant's wail,
soft click of a door closing? –
as the sound of his footsteps
swirls in his wake

just crossing Josephine.

Bruce Henricksen

Solitude

If you were here I'd say I'm sorry
for the bleary nights I spent in bars,
the fog building about our lives as it
built about my father's life
when I was young.

I see him now, on a windy
afternoon in November, maybe 1950.
Scraps tumble along the street,
mirroring the swift, high clouds, and
homeless men gather in doorways
to talk of freight trains, their words
punctuated by the squeak of corks,
their arms moving for warmth
like damaged wings.

In my mind I sit with him by a window
that frames a neon sign. The booth is
a mausoleum, its surfaces etched with
names and dates that ripple beneath
the hand, etched with the lonely beauty
of time passing in derelict places,
the beauty of disparate lives conspiring
to carve a text.

Outside the fog grows dark as any sea.
It parts from time to time to show
the ancient starlight—worlds beyond
worlds, the layers of time
beyond need.

In the orange glow of the neon, we listen
to Billy Eckstine sing "Solitude" on the juke.
I am home. I buy my father a beer and crack
the cellophane on a pack of Luckies. We talk,
slowly releasing the past from its silence.
I ask him if the drinking life began for him,
as it did for me, with the thrill of sex
lacing the air of jazz clubs and pool halls.
Or maybe for him it started with terror
in the carnage of the war,
his war.

Contemplative behind his Lucky, his words
riding the current of longing all drinkers
know, he tells his story. We smoke.
As the neon flickers, we turn from the
world like motes drifting in a shaft of light.
I carve my name.

But now is only fog. You are not
here, and yet you haunt me, Sandra,
as my father does, with memories
that will not die.

Street Lamps

I am nearer to the moon tonight
in our little town of sad eyes,
sagging rooftops and failed ankles,
uncomfortable pews in its church
polished as sailing ships,
docked museums at sea.

The park pavilion greys
before the neighborhood.
The palmist tent lies empty.
The sound of leaves no longer clicks
across the concrete courtyard.

Nightfall now embracing
the lone street lamps, sisters
in a quiet language from above.
The sky is working its memory,
be still, listen.

Evening Obscures Landscape

in the winter fog—
hushing night-birds,
silencing footfalls.
Dogs along the country lane
curl under porches,
leaving watchfulness
to a single-eyed lamppost.
The walker in the lane
counts pools of light
falling weakly to the ground:
his house recedes from form
dissembling
into grey and greyer still,
vanishing into a recollection of home.

dan of ben lomond

he was a guy with many names and just as
many social security numbers, with an uncanny ability
to make remarks that would slip past you, then later
could stop you cold. working undercover, a secret
poet merging in the shadows, slipping along walls and
through passages, moving by innate stealth. an honest
and straightforward friend he was though, despite his
being a natural thief.

like out of a mother goose tale, he was a
diminutive man, who had a diminutive wife, lived
in a diminutive house with a diminutive child, and a
diminutive cat. in addition to all that, he drove a most
diminutive car. as a rule he stole not from individuals,
but only from large corporations, businesses and the
government. the bigger the better. but in the case of
his morris minor he'd made an exception because it
reached out to him; he felt a recognition, a kinship. so,
contrary to his own code, he stole it off the street from
a private party and then transformed it miraculously.
he gave the car a fresh new appearance with many
coats of spray paint, all applied by aerosol cans with his
usual meticulous and professional care to the smallest
detail.

we liked swapping stories. i had been a social
worker down in l.a., and occasionally i'd reminisce about
my days in the department of social services and enjoyed
filling him in on how the whole thing worked. which
turned out to be a great inspiration to him. he opened
up a welfare case of his own under an alias, then two,
then three and a great many more. like a chain store he
was. i was astonished and a bit shaken to see what i had
unleashed. he would come to consult with me on these

matters and felt greatly in my debt.

so when the engine of my vw bus blew, he saw his chance to show his appreciation. this was an untimely disaster for me. he assured me that everything would be okay, not to worry. sure, easy for him to say, but i was living on food stamps while making wood objects such as carved boxes and hand mirrors with serpentine handles. i was building up my stock, as it were, before going into business. the point here being that i was broke and could not expect to buy a used or reconditioned vw engine with food stamps or, for that matter, with hand carved mirrors with serpentine handles. i felt devastated, done in; this was the end of my big enterprise.

then, two days later dan shows up in an old beat-up chevy truck, which was neither diminutive nor finely detailed. in the bed of the truck, however, there sits a cherry looking vw engine, with tubes and wires freshly snipped. it's yours, he says. how much? i ask, though of course my wallet is flat. and i consider that it may not even fit. trust me, he says, everything is in order. it's my treat and i'll help you put it in ... i owe you.

well, as you may guess, i'm not much of a mechanic, and so dan does most of the work. he goes about it like a surgeon, hardly getting his hands or clothes dirty, maybe a smudge here and there. being naturally curious about what things cost though, i ask him what he paid, thinking to myself i'd pay him back when i started raking in the bucks from the hand carved mirrors. he pokes his head out from under the bus and looks up at me quizzically, in a squint eyed way he had, as if he can't quite believe what he just heard. i *stole* it, he says, what d'ya think!

during a break for lunch, he tells me the story. over the hill in san jose, there's a used car lot he was familiar with. he sees a vw bug that *happens* to have the keys in the ignition, jumps in and drives it off. as

simple as that. he takes it to a place in the woods near
where he'd left his borrowed chevy truck, which he
had supplied with all the needed tools. then he yanks
the engine and shoves the bug over an overhang. you
shoved it off a cliff? yeah, he looks a little sheepish and
mumbles that he couldn't think of any other way. jesus,
i say, seeing the car crashing down into the woods and
thinking about a rusted out car i once came across in
a wooded ravine. i couldn't think of anything else, he
says and makes a face, i don't like to, you know, ... litter.

i've gotta say, the bus ran great.

then a couple months later he comes by one
afternoon. he didn't look too good, said his old lady
had left him, she'd moved in with another guy. a *jockey*,
he says, sort of spitting the word out on the floor. and
she took his little girl too, packed up and left him for a
jockey. he tells me all about it; as you might imagine, it
hit him pretty hard. then he wants me to come along
with him but won't say where or why. it's all a bit
mysterious.

by the time we get down there, to a little street
in ben lomond, near josephine street, it's evening and
all socked in with grey fog and wood smoke and a
dampness that cuts straight to the bone. he parks the
morris minor on a dead end street, sort of behind a
hulking redwood. as we walk back to the cross street,
he keeps squinting back as if to check and see if the car
can be seen.

we're walking along and suddenly he makes a
sweeping gesture to include all the encompassing fog.
can you feel it man? the spirit world? it's all around
us. a little further on he stops behind a black wet tree
trunk and motions towards a house across the street, a
little bungalow. that's it, he whispers behind his hand,
don't let them see you. that's where she's living with
the guy. the jockey. i come here a lot, every night. to

watch. this seems weird to me, because there's nothing
going on, the windows are dark and the house itself
looks ghostly in the fog. we stand there a long time. the
wet and cold is penetrating. faintly, off in the distance, i
hear a dog bark.

when we get back to my place, we sit in his snug
little car for a while, not saying anything at first. i
don't like my little girl being in that house with him,
he begins. i'm going get her away from them, i've seen
her alone after school. don't be an idiot, i say, they'll
nail you for kidnapping. she's mine, he says, and then
lets out a deep sigh, and then continues on. *i* could be a
jockey; i used to ride horses all the time. i sort of laugh
but then i realize he's serious.

not long after that he leaves town. and then i get
a call that he's got himself a job as an exercise boy, the
first step to becoming a jockey. and that's the last i hear
of him. but whenever it's a foggy night and i'm down
that way, down by josephine street, i can sort of feel the
spirit world he was talking about, especially when i go
by that house. i think whoever lived there has surely
gone by now. but it's like there's still something stuck
there behind the tree, unseen, watching that little house
with no lights on.

PAVEMENT ENDS

Andrei Guruianu

Brief Moments When It Was Possible

Not even a sidewalk to tarry on,
share some old news with a stranger.
Not a place for hands in pockets,
the common shrug of heavy shoulders
at things that cannot be helped—

out there on a stretch of bad road
tangled in distance and doubt.
And that all-too-familiar way back
endured too many times.

Mudhole

Life has no meaning. Right at the center of anything there's a big nothing, a hole large enough to drive a truck through. But nobody dies just because of that. My grandfather farmed for years around a mudhole right in the middle of the already meager acreage. A kind of curving ditch known as "the creek," though it seldom held any water. The mark of the harrow and the mark of the plow followed the contour of the bank making a pleasing pattern in the dirt. The way the lines of a poem are pleasing (something about seagulls, the sun going down and the dust behind the tractor, rising in a tall column so that it was visible even from the County Line Bar two miles away) or like bars of music which has no meaning either. Someone can take a perfectly good drinking song, turn it into an anthem. People enlist, and things get a whole lot worse. But meanwhile, back at the tavern, the music goes on and so does the drinking.

Translation

When I knew you were gone
I walked to where the pavement ends,
crept under the barbed wire and on
across the swale's soaked floor
shoulder to shoulder with spike-rush,
juncus. Greens with tips burnt rust
as if seed send-off was a fire,
a sun-pinched end. As if coupling
had torched them open. I wanted
to reach past the winking drifts—
fog, unanchored cobwebs. To climb
the solidity of red willow.
Blade of grass on my tongue—
from squirming under the wire?
The branch gave a bit to my weight.
I wanted to re-read your note.
But my hands were silt-caked.
Knees drenched in crushed dew
from ducking, kneeling under
the wandering threads of loss—
all silk, all drive—without a spot
to fasten on. When the sun began
to suck up mist's micro-drops,
every last one, a lone singer
caterwauled his lamentations
from behind the shifting screens.
Kis-ki-dee, Kis-ki-dee:
my back-pocket pages rendered with rhythm.
And there was no need to reopen them.

Joyce Odam

Diagnosis

So we are lost one more time in another vague corridor full of partitioned rooms, long curtains hanging on rods, someone directing us through each one. We talk of other things, not why we are here. You lean your head against a wall. I sag against a wall opposite yours.

We are immeasurably sad, ignorant of who we are about to be. You wear a long gray hospital robe now. I carry a purse full of your possessions; it is endlessly deep, it can hold everything. I stand and wait while you go into a room alone to disappear for an hour made of words.

I go where pictures on a wall whisper to the room where waiting is. A woman plunks down beside me carrying a lap T.V., tiny pictures that have harsh voices. She stares at them. I want her to leave. You are thinking of death now. Your head is full of it. My head is full of your thoughts, of which we do not speak.

Tracks

to my father on the anniversary of his death

At last the pavement ends.
Now if I lose your scent
I can follow your footprints.
You're still breathing in the fog,
your lungs ghostly and delicate
like white lilacs.

I don't care how many or what kind
have walked here, or run.
I only care about you,
your tracks fresh and firm,
as though you're nearly within reach.
Don't let me slow you down.
I will find you.

Bruce Henricksen

My Grandfather

One day my granddad took to wandering,
it didn't matter when or where.
He'd walk the road in morning fog,
or sit at noon beside a sullen pond.

And when the cattle pulled their shadows home
I'd see him come across a field,
the evening following behind
like some old dog he'd found along the way.

My mom said that her brother's death had made
him wander so. Perhaps the flight
of geese across October skies
told upon the air the tale of loss

with clarity no human words could reach,
with grace that no philosophy could teach.

Stephani Schaefer

When Old Men Die I Worry

How will they manage
after half a century of marriage
the long trek through the valley
with only a bedsheet
and the accumulated years?

Hems grimy, they'll arrive at the gate
and go in to a new bachelorhood.
Things won't look as shiny
as they did in the brochures.
For awhile it will help to play cards
in the lee of a cloud with the others.

Still, each man will wonder
what she is doing now,
if she will come soon
with a pile of fresh linen,
with rags and a pot of polish
for that shabby gate.

Meantime the wives,
tasting a bit of freedom after grief,
linger awhile.
Soon enough they'll worry too much,
pack the necessary items
and head up the valley themselves.

They're going to make things shine.
They're going to ask their men
to climb that cloud
and lie down with them in the sun.

Sometimes

Yesterday just out driving around and I ended up there
again seems like it happens every time I get in the car
that old road miles from town where the sign reads
pavement ends

I remember how me and John went there all the time in
the evenings riding in his car the one he bought from
his uncle for three hundred dollars we'd park out there
on the gravel road because there weren't any houses
out there only miles of cow pastures and nobody ever
bothered us

Sometimes we sat out there for hours searching for good
songs on the radio complaining to each other about
how terrible our parents were and how much we hated
our teachers talking about all the girls we thought were
cute

Sometimes when it rained a lot the road turned muddy
and we'd stop at the edge of the pavement because it
was such a mess I remember one time after a heavy
rain John decided he wasn't going to stop but started
driving through the mud and we ended up getting
stuck and had to get a farmer to come with his tractor
and pull us out

John was going to be a mechanic I remember the way
he talked about cars all the time how he told me he
wanted to go to school and learn how to work on race
cars I remember how excited he always got telling me
to just wait because one day he'd be on some famous
driver's pit crew

Sometimes we paid a college student to buy us a six-pack and we'd sit out there drinking I could always tell when John was feeling good because he started laughing at everything I said and he kept calling me man I remember this one time when we offered some guy ten bucks if he'd buy us some whiskey but when he handed us the bottle he gave us back our money laughing as he told us just to be careful and try not to get caught

And I keep returning to these same thoughts how long has John been gone now let's see it's almost three years already next month it'll be three years three years on the fifth and I still get angry about it I wake up in the middle of the night tears pouring down my face while I pound the mattress with my fists

Sometimes it feels like I can't breathe like I'm locked inside a box without any way of getting out and I can't help thinking I've missed something something he must have said to me maybe he tried calling me that night and I didn't hear the phone maybe I could've talked to him said something to him that would've made him change his mind I don't know I'm not sure about anything anymore

And then I get in the car because I don't feel like staying home and I drive out there again where the road looks the same to me the way it always did shouldn't it look different now and I don't understand why I still hear people laughing I don't know why I keep seeing children playing their faces alive and shining all of them bright and happy acting like nothing ever happened when I keep feeling like I just want to explode

Laura L. Hansen

Off the Map

I am a hollowed tree, a splitting oak,

feet dug in to a bit of scrubby land.

I am a shedding cattail, white-haired

and bent, on the shore of a county lake.

I am a seldom-used forestry road, all weed

and dust, an abandoned logging trail.

I am a track in the woods, stained with oil

where the 4-wheeler stopped a day or an hour ago.

I am a used-up gravel pit where teens partied

and petted last fall, leaving their mark in paint

and cans and one lost tennis shoe, the tilted

dead-end sign all pocked with gunshot wounds.

I am old and used and off the map, but

I am the place that everyone wants to go.

Lyle Daggett

flood warning

1.

in the bare oak branches a cloud of crows:
water rises unabated, the mud shores
fall away.

an age of short-selling and margin
leveraging, a time of challenges.
the nation is a kite that flies
before the storm.

through the long night an owl trills
in the sheltering fir limbs:
rattle of sky, whisperings, movement
behind windows.

2.

on the open road the road signs
are clawed marks that say nothing.
the horizon always hidden in mist.

"the american people will not shy
from any challenge, foreign
or domestic. we hold these truths
to be manifest: that the world
belongs to us."
sextant lines curving across the map,
basra, kandahar, bahía girón,
shipping lanes on a green painted ocean,
"here there be sea monsters."

turquoise hill specked with
                black-and-white cattle,
sound of a shotgun, whiff
                of silence, and
the shotgun sound again, as of
a metal door banging shut, or
                an explosion beside the highway.

3.

fog swirls mud-gray and jaundiced
at the end of the dirt road.
  in the breaking morning, in the wings
                of afternoon,
what augury is the light
                on the tails of wheat.
hanging by strings on a wire fence
  tin cans rattle in the wind.

signs of a gathering. plastic bottles,
crumpled newspapers, old tires
                piled by a shed.
heat rises from the marsh reeds,
under the river of rose gold light.
  two men sit in a row boat, waiting.
  lamps turn on by the house in blue dusk.
  sinewy, thin-faced, a woman
walks out to the mailbox, and stands
  looking out over the field, watching
  for a wind shift, a
                hinting, a hawk
                of knowledge.

Still Life with Dead Zone

1-

Pavement Ends

Single lane of hard packed, graded rock between fenced fields. Thick, intensifying ground fog covering the land, obscuring the caution sign, masking the way. Vision, at last light, no more than a few feet forward. Soon, the dark.

Maps without borders,
        unmarked trails
have no end.

Bent-to-the-earth signs say: Extreme Caution: Minefield Do Not Enter. A skull and crossed bones penciled beneath the words. Fields extending on either side of the road into the dark; the enclosing jungle trees beyond. The way on either side cratered from overhead bombing or from something explosive underneath. Large pits with still water inside. Other objects, as well. Soon, the dark.

Roadside Marker

Early morning still life with grazing cows. Sun bursting off last finger of ground fog drying the low, foraged grass. Budding trees just beyond wending wall of rock separating fields from drainage ditches and black topped road. Clipped lily on white cross by bare black limbed, skinned-of-bark tree. A scatter of car parts. Windshield glass.

> Confluence of shadow
> and fog, no light
> leaking through.

White stone marker embedded roadside indicates eighty-one kilometers to nowhere. Lifting ground fog and battlefield smoke envelop cratered highway littered with discarded gear: worn boots, torn rucksacks, unfolded blankets, ruptured canteens, tattered tents. Along the road, stunted trees, a long, thin barbed wire fence posted with warning signs, blackened fields of burnt elephant grass. Still life with dead zone.

3-

Blackbirds at Dusk

Bare tree outlined against a brushed-of-light sky. Blackbirds risen in flight. Cold, shifting wind suggests a freezing rain, sleet changing to snow. In the valley, the cleared field is collecting birds. Their gathering a strange collection of living matter among the desiccated stumps of summer. Long rows of them, newly sprouted like nightmares.

> Moon rise with
> > white comet tails;
> ghost light on an
> > empty outdoor stage

After the flight of birds, silence. Nothing moving among the dead, leafless trees, sheared to the stumps or broken into diseased humps, sprouting from the ground like the broken limbs of dead soldiers planted as a warning for those who follow after. The muffled steps of what comes after the night, their obscene bodies, their wings.

Flooded Road

Legacy of storm; a spontaneous inland sea. Reflections of immersed objects in still water: trees, tops of fence posts, vehicle roofs, antennae, tips as rigid as insect remains. Clear, cloudless sky cleansed of light.

Temporary bridges
        between two shores,
    water in the middle
            washing them away.

Fording the river in full combat gear. Foot soldiers holding their weapons diagonally overhead, walking, waist high, then chest high, some totally submerged. Only the rifles, still mostly dry, visible above the surging water.

Fog and Woodsmoke

    Evening haze with scent of cook stoves, fireplaces. Houses trimmed with decorative lights off-season; an almost unearthly glowing in near-night darkness. Still life with cracked blacktop and low hanging trees. The pulsing of the overhead wires almost audible. Nothing moving but the smoke. The haze. The strange rings of the overhead street lights.

    Dead air with black
        smoke; impossible
to breathe.

    Smoke from the burning thatched huts. The guts of cook fire spread on the hard packed earth: embers, overturned black pot, utensils for stirring, nearby. Last, spent remnants of location-marking flares amid the black, billowing smoke. A naked baby, sitting amid the wreckage, screaming.

Susan Kelly-DeWitt

Pavement Ends

So we need some sign,
some clear marker
to alert us the end
of the road as we know
it is indeed approaching
no U-turns allowed

What unrolls after that
(if anything does)
will be rough, most likely,
wheel ruts, stones,
crusted mud

Still—I'm hoping
we'll get lucky and
the foggy curtain inside
each molecule and atom
of flesh will lift

That the road might turn
into meadowfoams, goldfields,
blue eyed grasses.

ROADSIDE MARKER

Andrei Guruianu

We Are Memory

Stare at something long enough
and it disappears,
blends in with the scenery.

Listen to something long enough
and the sound begins to dissipate,
becomes muddled in the early morning fog.

Start walking away from it all
and it becomes arms, legs, limbs intertwined,
it becomes shadow, inseparable.

Joyce Odam

The Timing

It was the black cow under the gray crackle of sky in the cold field-light—the thundering back of sound—the soft reverberation into nothing—the slightest movement that the stillness knew. It was the far-off moment waiting to be this one. It was the timing.

The Wounded Tree

Death hit it hard. Enough
to wound it deep. It bled.
Death left a bright bouquet
nailed to the dying tree.

What is enough to say?
What is enough to say:

The branches shook. Leaves fell.
The bark could not reach 'round.
Black shadows stained the earth.

Jan Chronister

White Crosses

They stand stiffly along highways,
bookmarks in pages of miles
urging us to read
their stories.

A Wisconsin groom
leaves his bachelor party,
relieves himself in the road,
is struck and killed by his best man's truck.

High school boys
riding with clattering cans
collide with a train
leave behind two teams
each one man short.

Even in the Everglades,
Joe Tigertail, son of a Seminole guide,
has his name in big black letters
on a cross of lath strips painted white,
end of a father's story.

Open Memorial

Old coffee

Gets older

In the waiting room

Where we all wait.

In the corner by the tv

A Mexican girl touches

Her soldier's lips,

Her smile

So brave

For his future.

His future.

Your I-V bag

Half empty,

Half full,

Glitters beneath

Fluorescent tubes,

But the monitor

Is switched off.

Judith Pacht

The Closing

Call it a mercy, dark from the inside.
She can see it, the opening
& quickly the closing

that holds the numbing close,
keeps the other out –
splashes of sound

shaking light-like
through the pittosporum's
sulky leaves.

    What if I had said
    or you had said,
    here's money for the trip or
    why had I not said
    don't drive that thing
    or if you had said
    you must have said
    if I had only said
    & can we please
    just one time
    only this time
    can the ride be safe?
    can the plane land
    on the tarmac
    flaps up   wheels down?

    Maybe she'll be back.
    I ran after a girl—
    one shoulder hiked high,
    head tilted as though

listening as is her way,
hair sun-streaked, swinging
fast   just a glimpse
of course it was someone else

or maybe you'll say to him
wake up! blow liquid silk
the way you always do,
blow those round notes
from your bassoon,
& he'll wake up
whole   just as he was.

The closing again,
the erasure only
for the sleeping hours

not the crater-abyss
that sucks her in, even though
she holds the outer edge

hangs tight on the lip of it
resisting
fighting the pull

all the while looking into the dark,
the round, swirling, sucking,
insolent
abyss looking smack back
into her heart's eye.

Natalia Andrievskikh

High-pitched

The stark view of a postcard's quiet,
trees pretending to move
to the morning's crystal twitter.

And here, it is same old.
Cozy homes behind glass doors,
fireplaces turned into crematories,
framed grins beaming from every wall.

The heater's on 74, but I shiver.
A gape of no guilt hisses in empty rooms.

This desperate discomfort in the wrists,
an easy 'we' not to be continued.

Highway Signs

Stark, the white sticks crossed high
jut like the bones they represent
from rock piles or small graves by the roadside.

Plastic flowers loop in drunken abandon,
reminders of the absent drivers they replace
or huddle posey-like in brown string.

Ribbons blow to tatters in the wind,
red as blood pooled on the highway,
white as visible prayer.

Over a hill boom box blasting,
pickup lights flash across the crossed sticks,
disappear in waves of laughter, tossed cans.

Stephani Schaefer

Story

you don't know

the story
maybe tule fog, cows in the road

and now
this silent dawn

the flowered cross and stoic tree
the patchwork fence

the young grass
bending in the stream

mute tapestry

Roadside Marker

Someone riding low under moon or fog light?
Maybe... The curve too tight. Only asphalt knows
how fast breathing ran out that night.

For us: new morning:

Clouds overhead, drizzly compartments,
cold spacious apartments stacked along
the outline of the hills. Crows coast past,

fold themselves into a meadow's wild corners
like black handkerchiefs. Crying's done.
Doubters, the handkerchiefs have beaks,

talons, wings. *Look sharp now! Sometimes rain*
lives on for weeks inside the brain. Night: Day

again: A

-nother life in the leaves of grasses, scented
greens: *remembrancer.* A pictorial book,
The Americas, on the motel table before us.

Despite everything we must live. So we laugh
at the stellar jay out the window, who seems so
daft with his hops and his nips. Not daft, deft.
We call each breath lucky.

Nancy Paddock

Laid Bare

Cows look up with mild and fleeting interest
and go on pulling at the frail
green film of spring spread over the hills.

Fast cars passing may not notice the thin white
cross nailed to a roadside tree,
the bright permanence of flowers and grief
that mark a family's brokenhearted hope:
God loves you.

Its outer rings laid bare
as the hearts of those whose child
died here,
this tree that stopped a car, a life,
lives on to lay down new concentric rings.

New cells that feel no pain
begin to heal its wounds, restore
its tough, protective bark.

Rhonda

I pulled into this country store for gas, but then the engine wouldn't start. Sometimes it just needs a rest—time to cool down. Karin used to say it's chillin'. But it's no fun taking a whiz out in the middle of nowhere and then your car won't start. I decided to take a walk, so I went back in the store and bought a Snickers.

There was a picnic table about a quarter of a mile down the road with a trash barrel filled to the top. The table was chained to cement in the ground. I hoisted myself onto the table and put my feet on the bench, avoiding the bird shit with my butt. Across the road was this cross nailed to a tree, and behind the tree a couple of cows poked around in a field. One of them looked up and stared at me like I was something suspicious. The lookout cow. I tore the wrapper on the Snickers, but then decided to save it for later. I walked over to check out the cross. There were flowers and a handwritten sign stuck in behind the cross.

Rhonda　　Age 11
8/17/2009

I went back to hunch on the table and think about Karin. I probably looked like that statue of the man thinking, only he was naked. Anyway, me and Karin had been together three years. Pendulum years, I called them. On the good side, Karin would sober up. We'd throw out the empties and clean the ash trays. She'd get a pen and a pad of paper, and

we'd make plans, her pen always tapping as we
talked. In those good periods, she was all crucifixes
and rosaries. We'd go to mass and God would help.
Maybe He'd help us open that bike shop we'd talked
about. Karin could fix a bike like no one else. Maybe
we'd get the farm house we always wanted and even
have a kid.

But the cleaned up days never lasted. When I
said that once, she yelled at me for going down that
road. She said I was all dark roads and bad weather.
I said that life is just another kind of weather, that we
don't live intended lives. So we had issues. Everyone
has "issues" these days, even when it's just the same
old trash barrel of drunkenness and lies.

So the pendulum always swung the other way.
Maybe we'd drink quietly on the porch and watch
the evening rise like water between houses and down
the street. And there was this bar with a juke box
where she taught me to dance. I loved the tango,
especially the slow parts with the bandoneon and
violin yearning. Then we'd sit in a corner booth and
talk about the bars in Buenos Aires a hundred years
ago, when the tango was born among sailors and
prostitutes. We'd try to imagine their lonely lives,
the violence and longing of the men on shore and
of the women in the dark brothels, Karin's thoughts
flaring like matches in the dim light. She said that
abandoned things have their own special beauty.

Other nights she'd stumble off alone, yelling
after a fight, and later, with everything adrift,
I'd wander off too, wander off and wake up the
next morning with someone whose name I'd
forgotten. Wake up hearing rain on a strange roof

and watching the darkness leak away, leaving
the morning behind like something drowned.
Eventually, me and Karin would find our separate
ways home, with a blade of early light slicing through
the trees and under the shade in the kitchen. She'd
make coffee, and we'd whisper a few words—"You
okay?"—"Yeah, I'll survive." Even on the worst days
I wanted Karin. Love is fire, but I can't describe it.
Karin was like the weather, like wind that tears itself
apart until it's only scraps of wind here and there.

And Pete, Karin's dad, would come around with
his face like a headlight shouting about how I was
ruining his daughter's life. He was wide as a door,
and his cheeks hung below his jaw like tar melting.
He'd always bring up how I'd been in jail. He had a
black belt in resentment. Me and this other guy had
taken a trip to New Orleans and bought a boat and
went to Mexico for weed. I can't swim, but I figured
what the hell. To hear Pete, you'd think we were the
effing Taliban. One day, with Karin yelling her face
off, I chased Pete's fat ass away with my gun.

Our tango days were gone, and sunrise was
always a slap in the face. After that I left. I left in the
old blue Chevy with the starting issues. I'd bought
it for both of us. It had some rust, so the price was
good.

So I was sitting there on that picnic table with
the bird shit and my fist under my chin like in that
statue, except that I was also munching my Snickers
now. That same cow was looking at me while the
other one munched grass. Suspicious cow and
hungry cow. Pretty soon they'd haul their milk bags
back to the barn and evening would flow in like

water. It was time to wonder if the car would start. You don't want to be out on a strange road at night in a car that won't start. You want to be in a bar someplace, or a motel. I tossed the candy wrapper at the trash barrel. Maybe in a couple of minutes I'd toss out the empty knocking around under the car seat.

The cross by the pasture was in shadows now, and darkness flowed out of the tangled trees above the cross. I thought how the sign on the cross might as well say Stan and Karin, but it didn't. It said Rhonda.

Kathy Kieth

Every Little Death

tethers back to the big
ones: trail of crumbs half-

eaten by birds, but still
chaining into the woods—

back into the cold shadows
of yesterday's twilight—deep

into the loam under the trees
where the mushrooms grow

and the birds scutter for
insects: musty smell of old

compost, damp on
a papery skin...

Sally Allen McNall

What is the grass?

Stack them over there. The earth's ready.
The earth's always ready, and this job
is never done. Pretty soon we will get out
the jackhammers and start on the highways.
After that the cities. In the meantime,
when you're finished there, go back
for more. There are always more.

I promise you they will not become
more heavy, the smell won't get worse.
I promise you that the feeling you have,
that none of this is real, will go away.
You will begin to notice, as long, fine hair
falls over your arm, or as a child's head
fits into your hand, that you feel gentle.

You will feel you know something of the lives
you are lifting, moving, and saving.
For they are saved, in the most ordinary way.
The earth cannot turn away from us.

Rick Hilles

Larry Levis in Provincetown
(June, 2007)

This is how I am summoned from nothingness:
in faded cut offs, moonlighting at Connie's Bakery

where I keep reading Rilke to Jenny, the pastry chef,
who rolls her eyes, & blows flour into my tired face.

Beneath my limp baker's hat & stained white smock
I still wear my favorite Hawaiian shirt, the color

of bubble gum, absinthe & night. We are permitted
to choose but one companion for the great journey,

so Garcia Lorca is here with me;—we arrived last week
as "guest worker summer help." You'll be happy

to know that our work continues, as before, in Death.
Last night we finally had that conversation about

the moon, & mirrors—why they can't tell us
everything they see. We stood at an ivy-lined gate

two summers too late to deliver Stanley Kunitz our best
vermouth & news of Roethke and the other immortal poets

whose ranks by now, at long last, he's joined. Instead,
our poet of black notes took off his white tuxedo shirt

&, facing Stanley's last masterpiece, his front yard
garden, which still revises itself in preparation

for his return, Garcia Lorca revealed thumb-sized
lavender crescent moons, the eerie constellation

across his chest above the heart, the scars of bullet holes
from Franco's *Guardia Civil*; he told me everything—

from the faces of the firing squad to digging his own grave.
He says the landscape of his dreams has already drifted

from the Alhambra's gardens, wading pools, & almond groves
to the salt marsh at Black Fish Creek & the starlit wisteria

he affectionately calls, "These endlessly creeping vines
of strumpet braids!" And the delicate braids of Challah

we braid each day rise like old lovers awakening to our touch
restored. You should see the lean, aristocratic

hands of Garcia Lorca—they've never been so strong!
I didn't think such mortal progress was still possible for us.

Or that I would again be permitted access to the knowledge
that comes in a love amplified by the stirrings of the world.

And then I recognized something in the insistent, winding
taproot of an oak, which pierced me with the recognition

that is holy, & I felt the tug of gravity's widening spell.
So that even if Garcia Lorca and I are just scraping by

with all the others working for peanuts in high season,
to be alive again and living in a hot seaside town

is good as any afterlife
& probably our best chance at happiness.

Blackbirds at Dusk

Andrei Guruianu

Scattered Voices

Today I will go about
collecting all of my tired eyes
from where they've fallen over the years.
I will turn my back on the day,
go blind to this storm of angels
flying over the frozen ground
of an old monochrome dream.
I will sit under the trees
blistered with the sound of wings,
piling up the loose feathers
until I remember how to fly.

Haibun for Exile

for Okei, Wakamatsu Tea and Silk Farm Colony,
Gold Hill, CA 1870

Tea-tree and mulberry can be transplanted, but will they grow? She remembers mist over ocean, her ancestral land. Today, gray sky lowers with just the one horizon-line of light that keeps moving beyond her, west toward what was home. It's not quite spring here. They say a gnarled old apple breaks into fragile white blossom, pallid promise of fruit if wind and rain don't strip it bare. Is life nothing but weather and distance and loss?

Cherry trees dance
in their soft pink petal-sleeves –
it must be sunrise.

She listens to wild geese gathered in the meadow; they travel with the seasons, they'll be gone tomorrow into sky. This sky that still withholds its blessings. No sound. In town, down on the river, language is metallic among men who dredge the earth to sell its wares. Each man with his hand outstretched reaching for gold; eyes like coins. Beyond this house and barn, on the bald hilltop stands one bare oak, winter's skeleton. Could she ever root herself here and live happy as a tree?

Leafless, it blossoms
with wings, on each twig a bird.
Chorus of spring-song.

Magnificat

I wish I could carry a tune
for then I would write a simple song
about these blackbirds filling up a pearl
gray sky at dusk, along some river-edge
of winter, peppering the leafless
branches of an ash—

but since I was always instructed
I'd never be able to mouth or croon
a single melody, or hold any key
(except for the type with metal teeth,
to snug-fit the locked) I will have to hum
a poem's whole notes with my pen,
peck the syllables out of fog
and silence, nest them here

where a few words land like ink-
black birds along the notebook's blue
tributaries, its dry white estuaries.

Once I might have penciled them in
—*are they grackles? Or Brewer's…*
as Angels of Death, arriving to herald
some spiritual twilight, missing entirely
the way they're calligraphied like *yue fu*
on a shifting scroll;

how they're gathered together like
choir, or chorale—like busy notes in a Vivaldi
Gloria, a *Magnificat* by Bach; feather and beak
in a living tangle, yes—black bells, onyx

beads strung orderly and wild among so many
invisible rosaries of atoms, molecules, cells—
knitted close while darkness swells,
and a few late blossoms, though trampled
down, glisten on the sweet wet
planet beneath them.

Connie Wanek

Near Blackbirds

We fell in love near blackbirds, a tree full.
Among bare November branches
the birds became its fruit.

We couldn't trust blackbirds not to tell.
A kiss, and they took flight
all at once, circling the bell tower
like a black scarf caught in a wheel.

The wheel never stopped. We can say
that about a few good things.
We could see spring—last and next—
on every dark wing.

That Simple

A moment
is a bird's wing caught
in a cobweb
before it flies
I won't ask but
when you're carried away by memories
I'll listen
let me be a caring animal
wordless
because that's what I am
when your hands are cold
I'll cuddle up
it's that simple

Blackbirds In A Bare Tree At Dusk

Despite the miracle of collective consciousness,
life is filled with concerns about the ordinary:
light, fodder, plummeting temperatures.
So song becomes metallic, a series of twangs
and trills that function as connecting points
between the branching dendrons and ganglia.
One mind, wired with nerves in coordination,
knows to rub the heat back into its ruffled parts
by trapping air between feather and down.
So by the time the dome above is replete
with the burning hydrogen and hematite of stars,
each bird will be ready for a total silence
that holds the same fires within its cells.

In the language of rocks, every inch formed
or moved represents some thousand years.
In the language of birds, every feather-bone.

Sally Allen McNall

Winter

This small colony appears
still.
     Truly, it is restless as rain
ready to fall.
       Each bird perching
this moment,
       black fractals
like the bare spread tree,

like a moment in the mind.
         Like a tree
from stem to quiver in thinnest branching

the mind perches here,
       restless.

The Gathering

And so they come again this evening
to settle together in their favorite tree,
fifty or maybe twice that number,
the same black wings and yellow beaks
that lined the telephone wires last night
outside the hardware store, facing
the headwinds off the farmer's field,
watching the silo turn orange
in the dying light.

They have discovered the last country road,
the final stretch of field to horizon
in a land of big-box stores and parking lots,
the meeting places of humans.
They create their own city without walls,
money or vehicles, without worry about
marriage and divorce, kids, and doctors,
knowing only twig, seed, and worm,
not knowing when death will make a hundred
into ninety-nine, a gospel of the unafraid,
chattering, then stilled.

So now they huddle together,
talking of earth and rain,
whether it will be a good year for corn.
In the wind, which turns cold in late afternoon,
their iridescent ghosts remind us
that their conversation is untranslatable,
their love for berries and bark incomprehensible
from my late-spring window.

The fragility of lace on sky
veils a concert of small shrieking silhouettes,
a new definition of melancholy, of saying goodbye,
companionship without invitation, government,
neighborhood, marriage, or class, only
a favorite branch, wings, the sky, each other,
a convention of claw and wing
in one particular random tree.

Lisa J. Cihlar

There is a Day in August

The sky low and heavy
touching treetops, but holds back
the rain as if afraid of itself.

When the cats drowse all day
on the deck, when the flies
stumble through the air, aimless,
when the birds huddle quiet,
and the crickets chirp lullabies.

Blue Chicory and Queen Anne's Lace
tracing roadsides, leading nowhere
and everywhere.

I want to nap this day away,
eat soup prepared by someone
whose name I don't know, wear flannel.
I am cold in the August heat,
tempted by quilts and tea.

What melancholy is this?
A day between summer and autumn,
but too early, and tomorrow
it will have been a dream in the sunlight,
though the blackbirds
will be flocking up.

Steve Troyanovich

the brooding field

for Anthony Miklovic

And what dim angel weaves through the long moss there,
And what does it mean there
South of my darkness? You know.
Go, listen.
                        —James Wright

sometimes
a childhood voice
calls me to this field

beyond this lost last tree
beyond the blur of memory's
falling wings

near the crest of this field
near the childhood tree
weaves a long winter web
through recollection and illusion

nephew and uncle remain...
forever there

Doris Lueth Stengel

Bad News

A treeful of telegrams,
black-edged letters
come home to roost.
Hexes and charms
and most prayers
cannot hold them back.

Bad news travels fast
but stays too long.
The inevitable surprise
no surprise at all—
only its timing,
flying in from the gray.

The Pillow Tree

April 14, 1864
In camp, Jackson

Dearest Fay,

As ever when my mind is troubled, I turn to you. I turn to you, though the thoughts I confide may not be seemly or even manly. The great troubles of our times sweep through my soul like floodwaters. Peacetime restraints on what words are proper between a man and woman disappear like levees made of sugar or sand. My strength is not sufficient to withstand war's deluge without you, without your open mind, without your kindly soul abiding in sweet, southern darkness now.

I have lived the most terrible day of my life. I can only pray that providence holds nothing worse for me as this war proceeds. I offer no judgment on the fighting at Fort Pillow, only an account of what I saw. I trust you to draw truth from what transpired.

We came up to the works as dawn broke. A ditch and wide rampart are on a bluff above the Mississippi. Six cannon controlled approaches to its walls and there was a gunboat on the river below. Close to six hundred Yankees were within. Perhaps encouraged by their thick walls, some of the defenders called out taunts as our soldiers took positions in rifle pits. Our sharpshooters drifted to available high places and trees. Their bullets silenced the taunters.

General Forrest joined us at midmorning. He raised a flag of truce and called for the fort's immediate surrender. He offered his usual Cromwellian terms: surrender or die. The fort's commander asked for an hour to consider his options. He was given twenty minutes.

Our assault teams immediately crept forward. I don't know whose command initiated their stealthy advance through the moments of truce. When the twenty minutes were up, hundreds of our men crouched below the walls and in the ditch at their base.

A note from the Yankee commander was brought to General Forrest. He glanced at it and turned to the bugler. The bugler sounded the charge. Our soldiers at the base of the wall knelt, offered their backs as stepping stones. Soldiers concealed in the ditch leapt up, clambered over their fellows' backs and onto the parapet.

Curiously, this strong, solid fortress was defeated by its own design. The cannons could not be depressed to fire into the attackers. Our sharpshooters continued to sweep the wide parapet of defenders who tried to rise and fire. I scrambled forward and climbed up with my company. We fired a volley. Then the Yankees ran.

They ran down long slopes toward the river. Our soldiers ran behind and among them, killing as they went. Not quite six hundred federals, half of them Negroes, reached the river, turned and threw down their weapons.

My men were still under control. Sergeant Cabe ordered them to keep their weapons leveled and to slow down. They did. Others were not under control. Men from several companies continued firing. They screamed curses as they fired. Lieutenant S. from Company B ran among the men to my left. He shouted, "No quarter! No quarter, by Jesus! Kill these niggers! Kill them all!"

Others took up his cry. "Kill the niggers!" sounded from all sides. I heard a black soldier, already wounded in the foot, cry out for mercy as one of ours came near him. A shot in the face was his mercy. Some federals leapt into the river to swim for their lives. Spurred on by officers, a shooting contest began. It lasted for a few minutes until no targets remained.

My men stood uneasily, their eyes darting from one horror to the next. Some were appalled. Others shifted from foot to foot, eager to slip discipline's restraints. I told Sergeant Cabe to secure a number of federals cowering in front of us. He ordered the men forward. They gathered a dozen captives, three Negroes among them.

A man from another company suddenly darted between my soldiers and plunged his bayonet into the throat of a prisoner. The man uttered a strangled cry and fell. His attacker pulled the bayonet free and swung it toward the next man in line. Sergeant Cabe struck the weapon down with his musket. The wild-eyed man shouted, "It's orders, sergeant! We got to kill all the niggers here!"

Cabe glared at the man for a long moment and then spoke quietly, "Not these. Get back to your company, soldier." The man turned and shambled away. I ordered Cabe to form a cordon around the prisoners and remove them to the rear. I marched in front of our column so that none would question the legitimacy of our action.

We passed pools of blood and the leavings of unspeakable carnage all the way up that long slope. We passed out of the now open gate into the lesser chaos outside of the fort. I breathed deeply and raised my eyes as we escaped the scene of massacre. I raised my eyes and beheld a wonder.

A sycamore not far from the fort, lately a sharpshooter's perch, was filled with birds. Hundreds of blackbirds gripped every twig and branch with cold claws. Cabe stopped beside me. We stood in silence, staring for several moments. At last, he said, "It will be their turn once we leave."

Deep dread filled me as we turned and followed our men to the rear. I understood that each bird was a murder, that Jesus wept black tears for the wronged dead, that a mighty atonement must come.

Dear one, I awoke before this dawn from a dream which stained my soul. The tree of birds grows in my mind. I fear it always will. I am a disfigured man.

James

Nancy Paddock

Blackbirds at Dusk

As though caught in the net
a tree makes in the wind,
a thousand blackbirds settle thick
as last leaves on thin branches.

Silhouetted against gray sky,
they rest their wings, chatter
excitedly together,

a congregation of sojourners
just passing through—

as are we all. All drawn by hunger,
pulled by powers beyond our ken,

all caught up in the force field
of life's helpless wanderings.

FLOODED ROAD

Andrei Guruianu

Ordinary Miracle

Until this steel blue anger peels back,
the calm of sky and a windless pause.
It could've been like this, always,
only our memories so easily erased
that haunt the morning hour with regret.

How out of place the song of birds at such a time,
how little else to do but watch listen—
the urgency of daylight in their voice
and through some ordinary miracle
the knowledge that things never stay the same.

Stephani Schaefer

Hanging Out on High Ground

First sun we've seen in three weeks
of sideways wind and rain.

We'll wait.

The river hasn't crested yet,
every dip in the road filled with run-off.

We've seen our orchards toppled,
trailer parks in the valley underwater.

We'll wait.

After hanging out so long, what's one more night
sleeping in the car.

With what we've seen, anything
could be hidden under this sheet of sky.

In Their Language

for Cody

Last night in dream you spoke to me
in English – so unlike a dog, but that's how
dreams are.
        You reminded me of all those trips
we took together: In the bow of a john-boat, wind
in our face, an eastwind to bring you scent
draining off the mountains or rising
from underwater, all of August to a search-
dog's nose. On April hardpan, footprints dissolving
as you unraveled sun from shadow, the truth
of disappearances.
        Days and places superimposed
upon each other in sleep, as if I could peel away
layers to get at the stories: the man
who drowned; the woman who became rock-
fall. You reminded me: That last trip
                to the vet, I took your leash
with me home. Even in dream,
dogs don't complain.
        Maybe it wasn't English, after all,
but the common language
of leaving.

James Babbs

They Found Mary

They found Mary last week you know old-lady Mary who lived in the woods out there along the old dirt road that takes you down to Johnson's Pond we use to go swimming there when we were kids I remember when we caught a snapping turtle and threw it up on the shore somebody said if you cut off its head the body would continue to walk around but nobody wanted to be the one to do it so we tossed it back into the water

Some people called her Weird Mary claimed she stole little children and locked them in cages they said they heard she kept them in there fattening them up until she was ready to cut them up and make them into soup but I never believed any of that

You know who I'm talking about Crazy Mary who lived alone in that old house without any running water or electricity my Dad told me she was born in that house and lived there her entire life he said her house was full of old newspapers and magazines Mary had saved them for years and years he told me every room in the house was piled high with them and there was just this little path where she could get through

I think some people thought she was a witch or something I remember how kids would show up out there late at night smoking and drinking and doing all kinds of crazy things then they'd sneak up to her house and start pounding on the front door trying to see how close you could make it before she opened the door and caught you and if you didn't want to do it then everybody called you a chicken or something worse

  They found her last week drowned in the ditch near one of the flooded roads you know how much rain we've had around here lately the fields all full of water creeks overflowing their banks the other day I saw somebody's backyard and it looked like a lake

I guess some farmer was out driving around checking on his crops and he saw something floating in the water I guess he called the sheriff and the rescue squad went out there and found her they said it looked like she must have been there most of the night but nobody knows what she was doing out there or why she left her house in the first place and went out into the pouring rain

I heard the county's going to bury her somewhere near her parents' graves in that cemetery north of town I have a cousin buried out there and one of my aunts on my mother's side I guess Mary doesn't have any family and if nobody shows up to claim her property I heard they're just going to tear that old house down

Yesterday my dad showed me this box he wouldn't tell me where he got it from it was full of old photographs and he told me they were of Mary I saw what she looked like when she was just a little girl and then I saw her as a beautiful young woman with long blonde hair I saw Mary at a party surrounded by her friends I saw her dancing with some guy all dressed up and both of them were smiling there were streamers hanging from the ceiling and both of them looked really happy

Cleo Griffith

A Bit of Sky

From my kitchen window tonight
I saw a bit of sky turned story-book,
all vivid colors like a storm gone by,
like that we saw one time together,
above a simple flood on a country road
where, stranded, we had nothing to do
but finally speak again, not anxious to.
We edged our way around each other
as we edged around the flood,
marveled at the sky, and the reflection
across the water, the quieter part.
Why was it so beautiful just after its fearful stage,
and why did we forgive it so readily?
Tonight I saw that bit of sky, like that we saw,
and forgave the two of us again.

A Deserted Pearl

The day I tried to get to you
the road was flooded
with the reflection of the falling sky.

I saw many memories of you float on by
scrubbing themselves in the churning water
dissolving into the distance
where you waited
dehydrated and interned.

I remember you, remote as an
eroding island immersed in the moist sand
of parched tears and how the crooked path to your heart
was void of rain and clouded in grey.

I often go to that same place
where there used to be solid earth
a place I could stand
rooted as a pagoda tree
knowing my roots
the place where I could determine
the morning shoreline from my dark dreams.

It is all now a deluge
where I have learned
to swim in the deep currents of my heritage
discover primrose ripples of where I came from
identify with a diluted legacy
you, my father, left behind
after failing to endure
the remains of Manzanar.

Steve Troyanovich

Where Stars Touch

En la lluvia cabemos,
cercanos y distantes.
La lluvia es nuestro templo.

  – Rodolfo Alonso

i heard the loneliness in your voice
when you called out in the plundered night

 are all the roads to peace now lost?

centuries of bloody nightmares
flood this impassable road

homicidal acts of a sullen species lurk here
 a species most endangered and alone

love is a word...warm like rain
we belong in the rain

 i stand on the edge of night's porch
with a poem of wind and lost highways

 i listen to the silence of stone...
a sound that guards nothing

i long for the desperate embrace of stars

Lara Gularte

River in the Road

A flood of stillness
   widens the road,
      covers the solid line.

People in rubber boots
   move along the shoulder,
      spilling their identities.

The missing,
   a river of pulse beats
      weighted down by debris.

When full morning comes
   water opens like a gill,
      a salmon shoots into sunlight.

Road crews wake up,
   find rats and men
      living together in storm drains.

A woman leans into the street,
   her face a blossom falling
      to the surface of the water.

Rick Hilles

To Grow

(After Piet Hein)

There appeared before our eyes a tuft of grass
    on the earth.
Warm sunlight spread over it, as from spilled juice.
    Whatever it is, it grows.

It grows in sunlight, in sudden rains, in snow-squalls,
    in thunder storms.
Every little random treat, trinket, arbitrarily given sign
    gives it form.

Small charred bits from bonfires comingling in the air with
    compromised juices,
squeezed liquids, nectars, coming going through it bloom
    fresh airs and scents.

Another world appears out of the merest discarded gloom:
    an inviting bath
edged with green waist-high spearhead corn-silk stalks tipped
    with shriner's plumes.

It stretches out the hardest shells and encasings of seeds.
    It really does. It does.
Small hardly noticeable things, that weren't here before,
    now are coming through.

Softly created veins branch, leaf by leaf, into nervous systems
    out of mud.
Such fullness! And out of what? Nothing? ...Yet it happens.
    Minute tremors,

minute spasms, minute fissures, minute breaks, minute wounds,
    minute somersaults.
Out of shadow a newly awakening world rubs its eyes, waking,
    it eclipses the sun.

We have a lot of serious work ahead of us, we do, we really do,
    we two.
One needs to believe oneself so deserving, so rich, so strong:
    To grow.

Lisa J. Cihlar

After the Rains,
7.8 Inches on the Gauge

It happens every year,
dry dry dry hot and dry.
The grass yellows,
the corn leaves curl, tight and pointy,
the ground cracks in the gardens,
no matter how much water
hosed on them, it runs down
tiny dirt canyons,
chases out the crickets
hiding there,
never seems enough
to keep the wilt away.

Then it rains.
Not a slow, soft rain
to coddle every plant,
bring things gently back to life.
No. A hard rain.
An all night and into the next day,
wash the river over the banks,
invite the ducks into flooded fields,
kind of rain.
A weather advisory rain,
where the river crest comes,
tearing at trees dipping in the water,
pushing a red fiberglass canoe
to next county where it will be found,
pulled ashore
by a farm boy and his sister.
Their father says

they can keep it if no one answers the ad
he puts in the local shopper.
No one does.
Their mother is worried
one of her kids will drown
like the boy who lived one
farm over when she was a young girl.
The one she had a crush on,
kissed just once.

If she tells her husband,
he might not laugh,
he might even tell the kids
they can't use the canoe
unless he is with them.
But she won't tell him because she feels guilty.
Guilty that sometimes she wonders
what her life would have been like if that boy,
who liked to sing opera while milking cows,
hadn't drowned.

But the next big rain
catches the canoe, takes it away again.
The farmer's wife spends a whole day
humming a Puccini aria while canning tomatoes,
all cracked from too much rain.

Rob Davidson

Walter: Five Meditations

Blackbirds at Dusk

First, there are the birds Walter doesn't see: thoughts that leap off the branch, take wing, and are gone—the lightest of feelings. The birds he sees are memories not yet ready for flight, weighing down his branches.

Josephine, a girl he knows. Knew. He wants to write her story, to write of a night they sat in the corner of a bar for hours, her breath on his cheek, all lime-soaked and fucked up. She wanted him to say something. He couldn't say it, his tongue twisted in a knot. Last call: the bartender raised the lights. In the glare, Josephine narrowed her eyes. She left him with a table of empties.

In the story he wants to write, the lovers stand on the pavement outside as drinkers stumble like raindrops into the night. Smoke crawls up the side of her cheek. They move toward each other slowly. His nose brushes her ear; her breast is soft against his arm. In the story he wants to write, the man understands that this woman is a bird delicately poised for flight, already a wing unfolded. He speaks. He has things to say, words that indicate he is sensitive, aware, but not overly sentimental. Such qualities make him desirable. If a story is a power struggle, a little war between desire and fear, between him and her, the man wins. But Walter hasn't yet written this story.

One bird flew, and one remained. Failure, sharp as a beak.

Flooded Road

Road meets water. As usual, Walter lacks the thing he needs: a boat. Suddenly, it is the solution to many problems; if he had a boat, he might move freely on vast waters, navigating streams and rivers, crossing lakes and inland seas. If he had a boat, he'd transgress borders, ignoring petty geography and its attempts to shape his life. Everyone knows water shapes land! If he had a boat, he'd be its captain, the admiral of his own fleet. If he had a boat, he could trace all that water back to its source, that mysterious, burbling black spring: the fountainhead of many defeats, many lost years on dry land. He'd leap from his boat into that water, swimming down, down, down to the bottom, where he'd place his mouth over the gushing orifice, gorging himself. If he could, he'd swallow every last drop, draining the world of something, but of course one can never be certain what that might mean. One man's miracle is another's catastrophe.

Roadside Marker

A roadside marker, thinks Walter, is an exercise in revisionist history, an écriture of the heart. It's an attempt to say something to others that, no doubt, was misunderstood or unheard while the deceased was alive. Words, gestures, gifts left not for the dead, but for the living: to reassure them that they did what they were supposed to have done, that they loved as much as they could, that they cherished and valued and complimented the beloved when—and Walter knows this—the guy who drove his Ford into that tree last March was actually a real son of a bitch.

Walter's monument, should he build one, would not

look backward; there stands a litany of failure and despair, lost opportunities and half-realized goals. Walter's monument would be to the future, to the lives and possibilities still unborn and becoming, to the potential surrounding us, to the alternatives we can't yet embrace, the decisions we haven't yet the courage to make, the adventures we dream of and promise we'll attend to tomorrow. The idealized future is every ounce the lie that is the idealized past, but with one difference: there is that tender slice of possibility, the promise of what if, the knowledge that, with the next turn, the next blank page, the next girl you meet, your life might change.

Walter waits for something to happen, for when that something happens the past will be rewritten to anticipate what it couldn't have foretold—which is chance, really—sanctifying the present by making it inevitable.

Fog and Woodsmoke

In this town, you can stand in the middle of the street for hours and no one will hit you, no matter how badly you want it.

December, five a.m. The air smells of woodsmoke and diesel exhaust. Walter longs for snow; he imagines the first flake falling, tumbling in the air, its tines a dozen frail hands. But it rarely snows in this valley, where in winter the almond trees are skeletal and bare, even as the ground sprouts a blanket of emerald green grass. Fog covers everything in vague suggestion.

Soon he will return to his small cottage nestled beside the orchards. He'll toss another log into the woodstove, pour a cup of coffee, and sit down at his desk to do the only thing left to do. There are pages to be filled, words to be written, an empire of language waiting to rise. There is a Josephine waiting to be constructed: one who listens, loves, forgives. Walter serves her, humbly offering up a thousand words a day.

In a corner of his cottage sit his publications: a modest stack of chapbooks, journals, books. Walter shores these fragments against his ruins, etc., for it is this that gives shape to his existence, and purpose to his days. The world without words is the world unmade; it is not life that gives shape to art, but art that gives shape to life.

Pavement Ends

All pavement ends somewhere. Walter knows he's running out of road. He needs to make a turn, double back on himself, move in another direction. Or simply to stop. He keeps moving when stillness is the only sensible option, but then he's never been good at sitting still and just becoming. Each moment the perfect image of itself: that's not what Walter wants. He wants motion, the illusion of progress. Stasis kills the heart. If a mountain sat before him, he'd climb the mountain. A cloud of fog, he'd enter it. He's in it now. Has been for years. Coming or going? Walter rarely knows.

Joshua Clark

From Here On:
Reflections from Heart Like Water

Strange, what's strong, what's weak in a time of wind and water. Water rises, ravishes, then collapses right back into sleep. We do not know when it will rise again, cast confidence aside, and show us only what still stands. Now that the water is gone, homes are again washed clean of color, trees leafless and the roads cracked ash. Not a sound, not anywhere. Then noises come from the broken trees between levee and river. They lift into the cobalt twilight in three tiers. First there are the frogs, what must be hundreds of them, heavy, belching. Beneath that a cicada cries and cries and cries until another joins it and another and another and they stumble into a shrill rhythm. And below it all, holding these sounds and twilight itself up, are the other insects. I like to look up at the sky, especially now. There it is, always itself, always different, always recognizable, always beautiful. Violet haze hangs over everything and trees have become silhouettes. Here is the simplicity I long for: the butterfly opening and closing its wings, last light of evening scattered and shattered and shimmering upon the river, something to hold to, after the world here peeled into layers of sediment and sentiment. From here on, finding beauty will be the complex thing.

Permissions and Acknowledgements

Joshua Clark: "From Here On" is a new piece made up of selections from his book *Heart Like Water: Surviving Katrina and Life in its Disaster Zone*. Published by Free Press, a division of Simon & Schuster Inc. © 2007 by Joshua Clark. Permission granted by the author.

Joyce Odam: "Diagnosis" is from her chapbook *Peripherals*: *Prose Poems* (Rattlesnake Press) 2009. Permission granted by the author.

Judith Pacht; "Surface" was featured by *Writers at Work* as their January 2009 selection.

Louis Jenkins: "In the Streets" and "Mudhole" are from *Before You Know It: Prose Poems 1970-2005* (Will o' the Wisp Books). Copyright 2009 by Louis Jenkins. Permission granted by the author.

Rick Hilles: "Flashlight Story 2" is from *Brother Salvage*: *Poems by Rick Hilles*, © 2006. Reprinted by permission of the University of Pittsburgh Press. "Larry Levis in Provincetown" originally ran in the Fall 2007 issue of *Columbia Magazine*. Reprinted by permission of the magazine.

I want to thank Bruce Henricksen for inviting me to take on this project, Andrei Guruianu, Rob Davidson, and Susan Kelly-DeWitt for comments on the introduction, and thanks also to the group of early contributors who helped select the photos; you know who you are.

Author's Notes

Alan Catlin has been publishing poetry and fiction since the 70's. Since retiring from his job as a bartender he has been working on his fictional memoir, "Hours of Happiness" and a number of different poetry projects. Recent book publications include *Self-Portrait as the Artist Afraid of His Self-Portrait* and *Near Death in the Afternoon on Becker Street*, both from March Street Press.

Andrei Guruianu is a Romanian-born writer living in Naperville, Il. He teaches literature and creative writing at North Central College. Guruianu founded the literary journal *The Broome Review* (www.thebroomereview.com) and served as the Broome County, NY Poet Laureate 2009-2010. More at www.andreiguruianu.com.

Brigit Truex's poems have appeared in various journals, including *Atlanta Review, Canary, Native Literatures,* and *Manzanita*, as well as the anthologies *I Was Indian, Sacramento:100 Best Poems*, and *Nantucket*. Her latest collection is *A Counterpane Without* (Rattlesnake Press). She is founder of Red Fox Poets and currently lives in the Sierra foothills.

Bruce Henricksen is a former editor of *New Orleans Review*. His stories have appeared in various magazines and his collection, *Ticket to a Lonely Town*, received second-place mention for the Grace Paley Prize in 2005 and was published the following year. He co-edited the anthology *From the Other World: Poems in Memory of James Wright* (Lost Hills Books 2008). His novel, *After the Floods*, appeared in 2008 and is available on Amazon Kindle and from Lost Hills Books.

Cleo Griffith chairs the editorial board of *Song of the San Joaquin*. Her many awards include the 2008 Stanislaus Arts

Council Excellence In Arts Award for Literature, and she is with the STARS program as a poet in the schools. Publishing credits include: *Iodine, Main Street Rag, Cider Press Review, Quercus Review* and *Tiger's Eye.*

Connie Wanek's third collection of poems, *On Speaking Terms*, was released in January, 2010, from Copper Canyon Press. She was named a 2006 Witter Bynner fellow of the Library of Congress by Ted Kooser. Her work has appeared in *The Atlantic Monthly, Poetry, the Virginia Quarterly, Poetry East*, and many other journals. She lives in Duluth, Minnesota.

Donna Pucciani has published poetry in the U.S., U.K., Asia and Australia, in such diverse publications as *International Poetry Review, Journal of the American Medical Association, Christian Century, Li Po* and *The Pedestal.* Her books of poetry include *Chasing the Saints, Jumping Off the Train,* and *The Other Side of Thunder.* She is active in the Chicago poetry scene and serves as Vice President of the Poet's Club of Chicago.

Doris Lueth Stengel is a member of Heartland Poets in Brainerd, MN. She has served as president of both the League of Minnesota Poets and the National Federation of State Poetry Societies. Recently she received an Arts Grant to work on her second book of poetry.

eric (aka russell warren) nystrom has worked on the railroad as a lineman on a gandy gang, as a truck driver, a bookstore clerk, writer, social worker, school teacher, hypnotherapist, furniture refinisher, carpenter, sculptor, painter and printmaker. at this point in time he is not yet dead, though as anyone can see, he has no idea what to put in his bio.

Gordon Preston has had poems in *Blue Mesa Review, Cutbank, The Missouri Review, Rattle* and *Tar Wolf Review*...He was 54 when Finishing Line Press published his first chapbook, *Violins.* Now at 60, he still teaches reading and writing to the very young in Modesto California.

Jan Chronister has won awards from the Lake Superior Writers
Contest, the Wisconsin Fellowship of Poets, the Tallgrass Writers
Guild (IN), the Brainerd (MN) Writers Alliance, and the Bemidji
State University 2008 Diane Glancy Award for Poetry. Twelve of
her poems have been published as collaborations with printmakers
by the Northern Printmakers Alliance in Duluth, Minnesota. Her
chapbook *Target Practice* was published by Parallel Press in 2009.

James Babbs is not a real writer but he plays one on TV. He works
for the government but doesn't like to talk about it. He doesn't
like people who are rude. He likes it when the tomatoes start
ripening. He doesn't like okra and never did but he could eat lima
beans every day of the week. Some recent poems have appeared in
*Gutter Eloquence, Opium Poetry, The Panulaan Review, Zygote In My
Coffee* and *ZYX*.

Joshua Clark is the author of *Heart Like Water: Surviving
Katrina and Life in its Disaster Zone*, a finalist for the National
Book Critics Circle award. He is the founder of Light of New
Orleans Publishing, and has edited such books as *French Quarter
Fiction, Southern Fried Divorce, Louisiana: In Words, How You Can Kill
Al Qaeda (in 3 easy steps)*, and co-authored *You Are Your Own Gym*.

Joyce Odam, Canadian born, California raised. Edits *BREVITIES:
A Mini-Mag Of Minamalist Poems*. Most recent chapbooks, from
Rattlesnake Press: *Noir Love* (LittleBook #2) and *Peripherals* (Prose
Poems). She has a passion (amounting to a credo) for the relevance
of art in one's life.

Judith Pacht's two chapbooks, *Users Guide* and *St. Louis Suite*, were
published by Finishing Line Press; her full-length manuscript,
Summer Hunger, will be published by Tebot Bach in the fall of 2010.
A two- time Pushcart nominee, her work includes poems published
in *Ploughshares, Runes, Phoebe,* and *Cider Press Review*. Her poems
appear in numerous anthologies.

Kathy Kieth is from the Sacramento Valley of California, where she has been a musician and psychologist, has published extensively, and runs Rattlesnake Press.

Katy Brown is Social Work Supervisor with Adult Protective Services. She is a columnist for *Rattlesnake Review* and frequent contributor to *Medusa's Kitchen*. She has won awards in the Ina Coolbrith and Chaparral Poets contests. Her works, *The Quality of Light, A Poet's Book of Days*, and *Musings*, are available through Rattlesnake Press.

Lara Gularte was nominated by Bitter Oleander Press to *Best New Poet's 2010*. Her work has appeared or is forthcoming in such journals as *Bitter Oleander, Clackamas Literary Review, Eclipse, The Evansville Review, Permafrost, Watershed,* and the *Water-Stone Review*. She is an assistant poetry editor for *Narrative Magazine*.

Laura L. Hansen is the owner of Bookin' It, an independent bookstore in Little Falls, MN, where she lives with her two dogs Jackson and Lolly. You can find her store on-line at www. bookinitontheweb.com. She has two chapbooks in print: *Diving the Drop-Off* and *Why I Keep Rabbits: New and Selected Poems*.

Lisa J. Cihlar's work can be found in *Qarrtsiluni, Word Riot, elimae,* and *The Pedestal Magazine.* She was nominated for a Pushcart prize in 2008. Lisa is currently working on a book tentatively titled *When I Picked Up My Wings from the Dry Cleaner.* She lives in rural southern Wisconsin.

Lyle Daggett's books of poems include *The First Light Touches Me* (Red Dragonfly Press) and *The Idea of Legacy* (Musical Comedy Editions). His poems have appeared in *Pemmican, Blue Collar Review, Main Street Rag,* and other publications. He lives in Minneapolis.

Maya Khosla's poetry has been published in *The Literary Review, Wisconsin Review* and *Prairie Schooner,* among other journals. Her poetry collections are *Keel Bone* (Bear Star Press; Dorothy Brunsman Poetry Prize) and *Heart of the Tearing* (Red Dust Press).

Nancy Paddock's poems have appeared in many journals and anthologies, including *To Sing Along the Way* and *County Lines. Trust the Wild Heart* (Red Dragonfly Press) was a finalist for the 2006 Minnesota Book Award in poetry. Chapters from her memoir-in-progress were included in *Stardust and Fate: The Blueroad Reader.*

Natalia Andrievskikh is a Russian-born writer. She has been published in *Yellow Medicine Review* and appeared in the anthology *Twenty Years After the Fall* (Parlor City Press, 2010). She is working on her PhD in Comparative Literature at SUNY Binghamton, where she came as a Fulbright scholar.

Patricia Wellingham-Jones is published in many journals and Internet magazines, including *HazMat Review, Ibbetson Street, Edgz* and *Wicked Alice.* Poetry chapbooks include *Don't Turn Away: poems about breast cancer, End-Cycle, Voices on the Land* and *Hormone Stew.*

Rick Hilles' *BROTHER SALVAGE* won the 2005 Agnes Lynch Starrett Poetry Prize (University of Pittsburgh Press) and was named the 2006 Poetry Book of the Year by ForeWord Magazine. He's a recent recipient of a Whiting Writers' Award and a Camargo Fellowship, and his work has appeared in *Harper's, Poetry, The Nation,* and *The New Republic.* He is an assistant professor of English at Vanderbilt University.

Rob Davidson is the author of *Field Observations: Stories* (Missouri, 2001) which won the Maria Thomas Fiction Award, and *The Master and the Dean: The Literary Criticism of Henry James and William Dean Howells* (Missouri, 2005). His novella "Criminals" won the 2009 Camber Press Fiction Chapbook Award, judged by Ron Carlson, and will be published as a limited edition chapbook. He teaches literature and writing at California State University, Chico.

Robert Walton is a life-long rock-climber and mountaineer. His writing about climbing has been published in the Sierra Club's *Ascent.* A dramatization of his story, "Three's a Crowd", was broadcast on KUSF on November 22nd, 2006 and subsequently on NPR. His "Don Francisco Rides to La Paz" won first place in the Saturday writers 2008 short story contest. Most recently, his *Chaos Gate*, a novel for young adults, won they 2010 Yorkshire Publishing competition and will be out in October.

Sally Allen McNall has lived and written and taught in Kansas, New Zealand, Ohio and California. Her chapbook, *How to Behave at the Zoo and Other Lessons*, was a winner of the State Street Press competition. Her first book manuscript, *Rescue*, won the Backwaters Press Prize. A chapbook, *Trying to write a poem without the word blood in it*, came out in 2005. Her latest book, *Where Once*, was published by Main Street Rag in 2010.

Stephani Schaefer is a poet and photographer with work in *Brevities, Song of the San Joaquin, Rattlesnake Review, EDGZ, Lilliput Review*, and others. She co-edited and provided cover art for the anthology *The Heart's Content* (Hypoplastic Right Hearts, 2009) and provided the photographs for this book.

Steve Troyanovich's work has appeared in *From the Other World: poems in memory of James Wright* (Lost Hills Books, 2008) and in many other publications including: *Arabesques Review, Poetry Salzburg Review,* and *The Dawntreader*. He was co-editor of the fantasy poetry anthology, *Omniumgathum* (Stygian Isles Press, 1976) and author of *Dream Dealers and Other Stories* (Triton Press, 1978).

Susan Kelly-DeWitt's most recent book is *The Fortunate Islands* (Marick Press, 2008). Her work appears in anthologies such as *Highway 99* and *Claiming the Spirit Within*, and most recently *The Autumn House Anthology of Contemporary American Poetry.*

Taylor Graham is a volunteer search-and-rescue dog handler in the Sierra Nevada. Her poems have appeared in *The Iowa Review, Southern Humanities Review*, and elsewhere. She's included in the anthology *California Poetry: From the Gold Rush to the Present*. Her book *The Downstairs Dance Floor* was awarded the Robert Phillips Poetry Chapbook Prize. Her latest – *Walking with Elihu, poems on Elihu Burritt, the Learned Blacksmith* – is available on Amazon.

Tazuo Basho Yamaguchi has earned a national reputation as a poet, educator, Haiku master and filmmaker for a full decade through his solo tours, his films, and his "provocative" poetry workouts and workshops that guide the voices of youth to the elders. For More Info: ThePoetTazuo.com

About the Editor

Stephani Schaefer is a graphic artist, photographer and poet who finds her material while exploring the back roads and wetlands of the Sacramento River Valley in northern California. The photos in this book were taken in Los Molinos not far from her home.

She may be contacted at schaefer.stephani@gmail.com.

Lost Hills Books
WWW.LOSTHILLSBKS.COM

Other Titles from Lost Hills Books

From the Other World: Poems in Memory of James Wright, ed. Bruce Henricksen and Robert Johnson.

Estuary, poems by Barbary Chapel.

Tumbled Dry, poems by Charmaine Donovan.

South First and Lakefront, poems by Dennis Herschbach.

Staying Blue, poems by Gibbons Ruark.

After the Floods, novel by Bruce Henricksen.

To purchase, to read reviews, to see author pictures, and to learn about coming events, come to the hills at www.losthillsbks.com.